The
ICKY BUG
Counting Book

by Jerry Pallotta
Title by Neil Pallotta
Illustrated by Ralph Masiello

Charlesbridge

This book is dedicated to Edward G. Taylor.

Published by
Charlesbridge Publishing
85 Main Street
Watertown, MA 02172
(617) 926-0329

Library of Congress
Catalog Card Number 91-73360
ISBN 0-88106-496-3 (softcover)
ISBN 0-88106-497-1 (hardcover)

Printed in the United States of America
(sc) 10 9 8 7 6 5 4 3 2
(hc) 10 9 8 7 6 5 4 3 2

Ralph would like to dedicate the illustrations
to his wife, Dawn, and his daughter, Alexa.

Books by Jerry Pallotta:
The Icky Bug Alphabet Book
The Bird Alphabet Book
The Ocean Alphabet Book
The Flower Alphabet Book
The Yucky Reptile Alphabet Book
The Frog Alphabet Book
The Furry Alphabet Book
The Dinosaur Alphabet Book
The Underwater Alphabet Book
Going Lobstering
The Icky Bug Counting Book

Although most people consider every
creature in this book a bug, in fact, only
the Stinkbug, Kissing Bug, Oak Tree-
hopper, and Cicada are true bugs. The
Elegant Crab Spider and Daddy Longlegs
are arachnids. The Millipede is a diplopod.
The Pillbug is a crustacean. The rest,
including the true bugs, are insects.

Thank you Icky Bug Man.

0 zero

Most counting books start with the number one.
This book starts with none. Zero! Zero is a number.
There are zero bugs on this page.

1 one

Here is one Zebra Swallowtail Butterfly on a flower. Butterflies taste things with their feet. Can you imagine if people tasted their ice cream cones with their feet?

two

2

Flies may have gotten
their name because they fly
so well. On this page there are
two Yellowjacket Flies. They are
often mistaken for Yellowjacket
Wasps, but Yellowjacket Flies do not sting.

3 three

Three Elegant Crab Spiders
are walking on a branch looking
for insects to eat. It is hard to believe
anyone would name a spider "Elegant." All
spiders have eight legs, and most even have eight eyes.

4

four

Four Paper Wasps are building their nests. Paper Wasps chew on wood. They mix the chewed-up wood with their saliva to make paper nests. Wasps could make paper thousands of years before people learned how to.

5   five

Butterflies rest with their wings straight up. Here we have five Viceroy Butterflies. Birds do not eat these good-tasting butterflies because they look almost exactly like bad-tasting Monarch Butterflies. I wouldn't want to eat either one, would you?

six 6

They are hard to find, but there are
six Underwing Moths on this page.
Underwings hide by blending in
with the bark of trees. Every
now and then, they show
their colorful underwings.
All moths rest with
their wings down.

7

seven

It's time to count. One, two, three, four, five, six, seven. Here are seven Trap-jaw Ants. Ouch! Ouch! Ouch! They capture other bugs with their huge jaws.

eight 8

Eight bright green Stinkbugs are crawling on these branches. If a person picks up a Stinkbug, his or her hands will smell awful! Stinkbug is a perfect name for these smelly bugs.

9
nine

Nine colorful Red Milkweed
Beetles are walking on these
leaves. These bugs lay their eggs
on milkweed plants. Thousands
and thousands of different kinds of
beetles live all over the world.

ten

10

There is an old saying: "Everyone wants
to be a butterfly, but nobody wants to be
a caterpillar." Every butterfly was a caterpillar
before it became a butterfly. On this page there
are ten Question Mark Caterpillars. They will
become ten Question Mark Butterflies.
Why are they called Question Marks?
That's a good question!

11 eleven

Pillbugs are not really bugs. These eleven Pillbugs are crustaceans, just as lobsters and crabs are crustaceans. If you touch a Pillbug, it will roll itself up into a ball and look like a little pill. Pillbugs also look like tiny armadillos.

Treehoppers are great jumpers.
These twelve Oak Treehoppers
look like thorns. Their shape
allows them to hide near real
thorns. It also makes them hard
to count.

12

twelve

13
thirteen

On this page are thirteen Nut Weevils.
Weevils are bugs that have very long mouths.
Many people have heard of Boll Weevils,
the bugs that ruin cotton crops. Not many
people have heard of Nut Weevils. Would
you like it if your first name were Nut?

fourteen 14

Fourteen Millipedes are running around. Gardeners welcome Millipedes because they chew up wood and turn it into plant food. The word Millipede means "one thousand legs." Millipedes do not really have one thousand legs, but they do have a lot of legs.

15
fifteen

One, two, three, four, five, six, seven, eight, nine, ten, eleven, twelve, thirteen, fourteen, fifteen Longhorn Beetles. They do not really have horns, they have long antennas. It would be pretty funny if longhorn cattle had antennas.

When you are counting on this page, do not count the dead grasshopper.

These sixteen bugs are called Kissing Bugs, but they do not kiss other bugs. They bite other bugs in the face, usually around the mouth. Kissing Bugs are not very nice.

16

sixteen

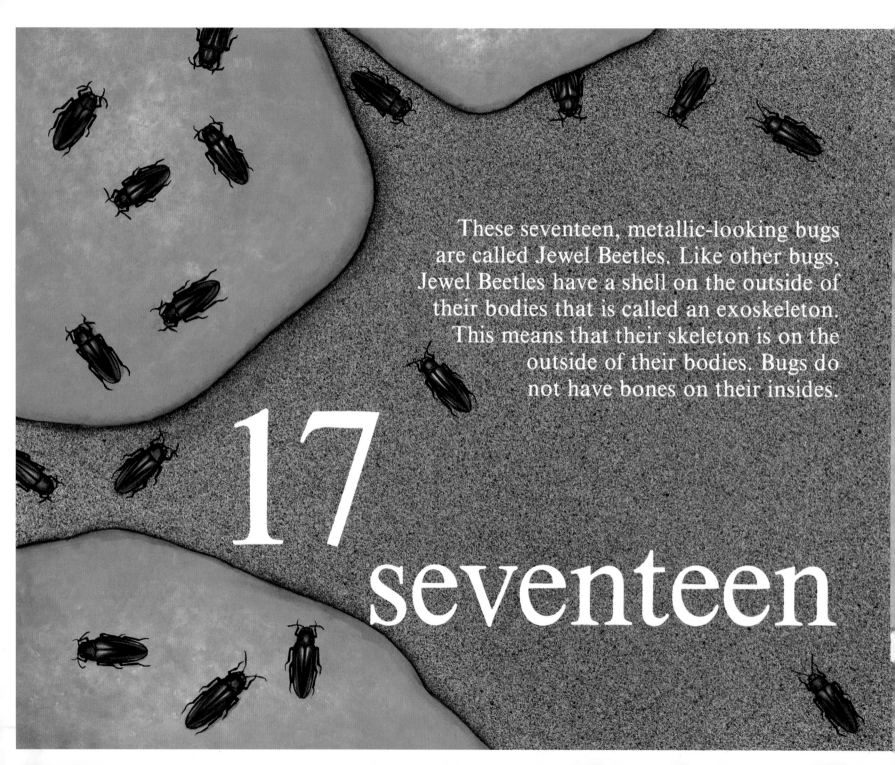

These seventeen, metallic-looking bugs are called Jewel Beetles. Like other bugs, Jewel Beetles have a shell on the outside of their bodies that is called an exoskeleton. This means that their skeleton is on the outside of their bodies. Bugs do not have bones on their insides.

17

seventeen

eighteen 18

Here are eighteen Ironclad Beetles. They probably got their name because their bodies are so hard. Their white bodies with black spots make them look like the dogs that are called Dalmatians.

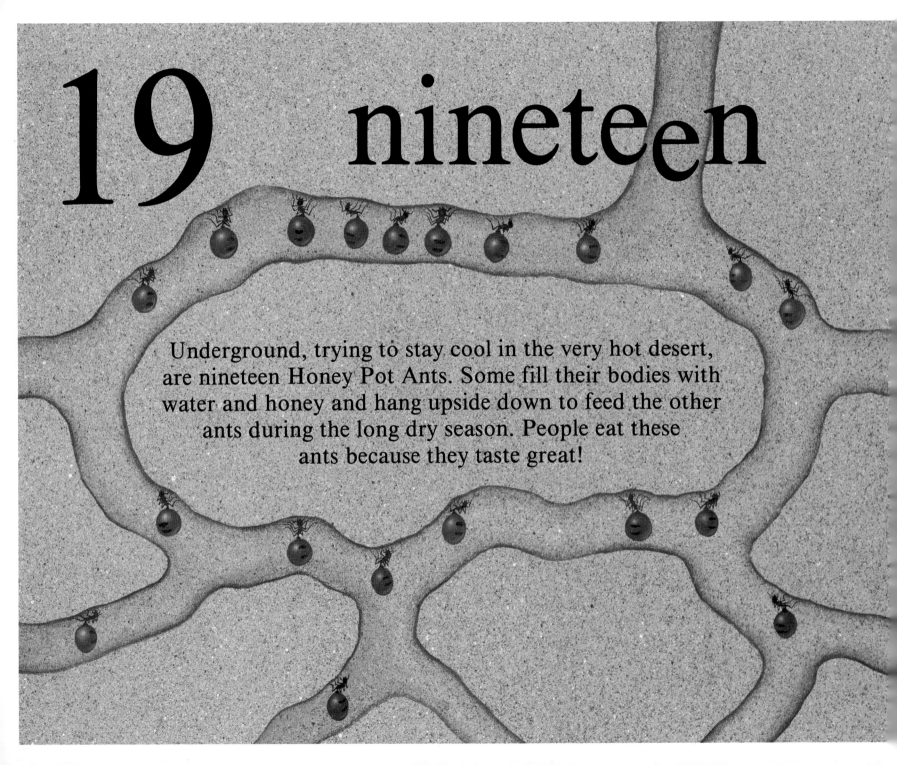

19 nineteen

Underground, trying to stay cool in the very hot desert, are nineteen Honey Pot Ants. Some fill their bodies with water and honey and hang upside down to feed the other ants during the long dry season. People eat these ants because they taste great!

Here are twenty Glowworms, glowing in the dark. Glowworms are not worms. Years ago, anything that was long and wiggly was called a worm. These Glowworms are really beetles.

20
twenty

twenty-one
21

How did this dog sneak into this book? This Irish setter has twenty-one Fleas. You cannot count them because Fleas are so tiny that they are really hard to find. This dog should take a bath and get a flea collar.

twenty-two 22

Twenty-two Eyed Click Beetles are on this page.
Click Beetles flip themselves over by snapping their bodies.
They make a clicking sound when they flip over.
Click! Some flip as high as four or five inches!

23 twenty-three

Can you count the twenty-three Daddy Longlegs on this page? Although these creatures have eight legs, they are not spiders. Has anyone ever seen a Mommy Longlegs?

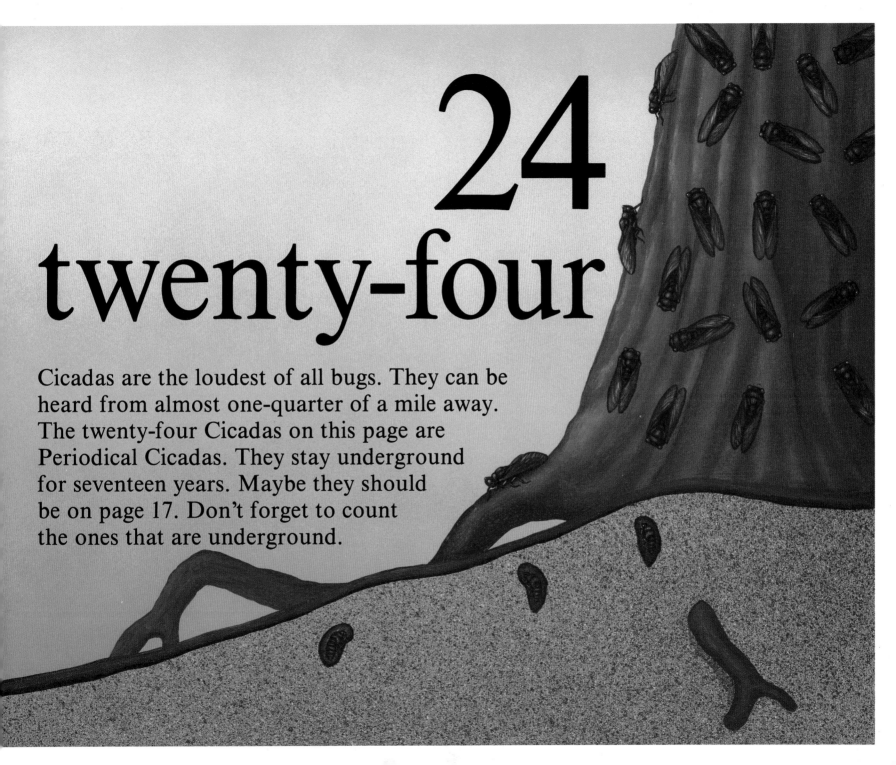

24
twenty-four

Cicadas are the loudest of all bugs. They can be heard from almost one-quarter of a mile away. The twenty-four Cicadas on this page are Periodical Cicadas. They stay underground for seventeen years. Maybe they should be on page 17. Don't forget to count the ones that are underground.

25

Twenty-five Blister Beetles are walking
around on the desert sand. Blister Beetles
squirt a liquid that causes blisters on people.
Yuck! Icky!

twenty-five

Actually, Blister Beetles are not that bad. Some are used to make medicines that help people.

26

Count the twenty-six Army Ants
on this branch. They must be lost.
Army Ants are usually seen in
groups of five hundred thousand to
three-quarters of a million at a time.

twenty-six

Army Ants have no permanent nests because they are almost always moving. Small animals, such as mice, snakes, lizards, and other bugs, run as fast as they can to escape the marching Army Ants.

Did you wonder why this book counts up to the number twenty-six? Here is a clue: the Elegant Crab Spider has the scientific name *Xysticus elegans*. Shh, shh. If you know, don't tell anyone!

By the way, this butterfly is called an Eighty-eight Butterfly. It really does have the number 88 on the underside of its wings just as the Question Mark Butterfly has a white question mark on the underside of its wings. The Eighty-eight is a perfect insect for the *Icky Bug Counting Book*.

(The secret reason this book counts up to twenty-six is that there is one icky bug for each letter of the alphabet — backwards!)